FOCUS
MASTERY

*Master Your Attention,
Ignore Distractions, Make
Better Decisions Faster and
Accelerate Your Success*

SOM BATHLA

www.sombathla.com

Your Free Gift Bundle

As a token of my thanks for taking out time to read my book, I would like to offer you a gift pack:

<u>Click and Download your Free Gift Bundle Below</u>

You can also grab your FREE GIFT BUNDLE through this below URL:

http://sombathla.com/freegiftbundle

More Books by Som Bathla

(All books available at www.amazon.com and also at www.sombathla.com)

1. **Procrastination NO MORE!: 27 Effective Strategies to Stop Procrastination, Increase Productivity and Get Things Done in Less Time**

Procrastination- NO MORE! is written to comprehensively address the menace of procrastination. It goes on to explain the key reasons, mindset problems and the language, which causes one to procrastinate. The book focuses on mindset development and suggests effective strategies to beat procrastination.

In this **holistic blueprint**:

- **5 Mindset Bugs** which rule the Procrastinator's mind and how these differ from a non-procrastinator's mindset with a focus on mindset development.
- **11 key Reasons why People Procrastinate** (You will definitely find yours)
- Lastly, the most actionable portion of this book, **27 time-tested strategies**, implemented by the productivity stars to beat procrastination and rock their

performance to the next best level. And how can you learn these strategies?

- Learn the less heard principles like "**Step One-Clarity Rule**" and how to quickly start anything despite feeling overwhelmed.
- You will understand how "**Just in Time**" approach works wonder **instead of "Just in Case"** approach.
- You will learn how to **mitigate digital distractions by 75% instantly** by following practical strategies
- And much more practical and useful action steps.

2. <u>**Master Your Day- Design Your Life: Develop Growth Mindset, Build Routines to Level-Up your Day, Deal Smartly with Outside World and Craft Your Dream Life**</u>

This book on winning your days covers:

- You would learn **what types of mindset** will simply design your days for extreme positivity and productivity.
- Learn the **best rituals** to imbibe in your mind and master your day.
- Schedule **effective daily reminders** for achieving a calm and focused day.
- You will learn the best strategies to deal smartly with outside environment including "**CTT Technique**"

- Learn **how to effectively handle the adverse work pressures** and how to keep going in the face of failures.
- Understand the **3 minutes/3 Hours/3 Days Rule** for getting surrounded with achievers.
- If you are an introvert, no worries, learn how to be **"Selectively Social"**
- Learn the least heard **18:40:60 Rule** for prompting you to become more authentic.
- Learn the **PDF Principle** for enhancing your productivity

3. **The 30 Hour Day: Develop Achiever's Mindset and Habits, Work Smarter and Still Create Time For Things That Matter**

This Productivity Book will help you:

- To feel more **in control of your personal and working life**.
- Provide easy to follow techniques on **how to stop procrastinating** and find a permanent cure to procrastination.
- Feel like **creating few more hours in your day** with simple mental tweaks.
- Work smarter not harder
- Understand **how to be fearless in all situations**.
- Reduce Stress and anxiety
- Creating new **healthy and successful mindsets and habits** for life.

- Re-wiring your brain by creating new neuro-pathways to think differently and keep moving further without any stress.

4. **<u>The Quoted Life: 223 Best Inspirational and Motivational Quotes on Success, Mindset, Confidence, Learning, Persistence, Motivation and Happiness</u>**

This book firstly explains the significance of inspirational quotes and motivational quotes in our lives. It explains why these quotes and saying helps us in developing resourceful mindsets and improving confidence. Due to following reasons, these quotes are important:

- These are **originated from our role models**.
- We can relate ourselves
- Consistent reminders of **what is possible**.
- Helps instantly **encounter negative feelings.**
- Daily **mental spark**
- Help creation of new belief System
- Develop new perspective to see the world in an abundant way.

So, if you are looking for your daily dose of motivation and inspiration to get success faster, develop a positive mindset, build-up your confidence, this book is for you. This book will give you one liner quotes on staying persistent, the significance of life long earning and quick phrases on happiness.

For More details and subscribing to the newsletter, please visit www.sombathla.com

CONTENTS:

PART I: INTRODUCTION

*****

Just think about your personal experience while doing your important tasks!

- Do you struggle to put your all energy and focus on the work at hand?
- Do you get distracted with every other ringtone or notification on your smart phone and switch from your work?
- Do you get tempted to engage in gossiping or office conversation more than often at the cost of hampering your work?
- Do you think that your environment is not conducive for you to put focussed efforts into your work?

Chances are that either you would have felt it about yourself or at least observed it in your surroundings.

I have personally experienced it many times and also seen people around in the corporate world suffering from a deficit of focus most of the times. Not only in the corporate world. In every area of your life, if you see around, it has generally become too difficult to stay attentive for a longer time.

The modern technology and the communication/social media tools have greatly added to the woes to the already distracted society.

Try to compare today's world with just one generation before only and you would note the difference.

The difference is clearly in terms of the number of distraction added to our lives. The old generation just had a television at their house. Some of you may ask your grandparents and they will tell you that it used to be a luxury to have television at home. Also, there were only fixed line telephones at houses or at the office. This way, people were approachable only when they were stationed at particular places and otherwise not.

The point I am trying to make here is that the number of distractions in the past were very limited. Therefore, there was a scope that if you put some efforts with discipline, you would have been able to focus on the work at hand. At least, the technology was not so deeply pervasive in people's lives in those days.

A Look at Today's Modern Day Life

You would agree that the modern day technology has given all of us numerous advantages. The technology has tied the world so closely that the world seems to be a global shopping complex itself. The advent of the internet has further made this world ultra-connected. The global trade and communication means are so much seamless that you don't realize the distance of thousands of miles. The exchange of ideas is super quick and instantaneous as compared to one or two generations ago.

But, this same technology has produced too many side effects as well. These side-effects are clearly the focus drainer and very frequently distract us from our important works. Below is a list of the few side effects that have come with the new technology.

   a. Every morning you are inundated with an endless number of emails to be responded on yesterday basis.

b. You mobile phone, which is not merely a talking instrument, has become a mini-computer in your pocket on a daily basis, throwing all kinds of news alerts and updates every few seconds.

c. Your social media networks are frequently bombarding you with news feeds and funny pics and videos of your friends every now and then.

d. The automatic notifications on the apps installed on your phone, keep on blinking or beeping to you 100 times a day.

What does all this lead to?

Obviously, sitting calmly and focussing on your important deliverables has become much more straining these days on two counts.

First of all, one has to spend enough amount of willpower and energy to stay focused on the complex project.

Secondly, the energy spent in staying away from all such distractions also drains much of your energy.

Even if you have cast-iron willpower, the mere fact that the Internet is lying in wait on your computer takes a toll on your work performance. The very act of resisting temptations eats up concentration and leaves you mentally depleted. There was a study conducted in 2011 at the University of Copenhagen to assess the consumption of energy and will power in killing temptation to avoid looking at your messages. The study showed that two sets of people were given same work and also the access to some video.

In this study, one set of people was shown the video directly and the other group was given the access to the play video button, but they couldn't play it.

After this test, both the groups were given the same additional tasks to be completed. The results showed that the latter group which was told to resist the temptation to watch the videos performed worse than the former one.

To put it simply, while focussing on your important tasks in itself requires a lot of discipline and efforts, additionally keeping oneself away from too many distractions makes the job of focussing on the key deliverable much more difficult.

How Does Lack Of Focus Affect Your Life?

You might think that few distractions here and there are okay, even while doing your important task.

You might also give an argument that life is too short not to enjoy on things coming our way or you might try to justify your distractions in any other manner.

But the scientific fact behind all this reasoning and justifications is that human brain is structured this way to immediately welcome any pleasure or any form of instant gratification. Every distraction from work seems to be an instant pleasure tool for us.

So, in the short term, it might appear to be a lighter issue, but in the long run, the inability to focus on our key deliverables and goals has a negative impact on almost all areas of our lives.

Let's Try To Understand This With An Example Of The Sport Of Golf.

When the Golfer raises his stick to hit the ball, two things are really very important. First, the amount of force to be applied so that it is optimal for the distance to be covered by the ball. Secondly and most importantly, the direction in which the ball should be hit.

Please note that no matter what optimal force you apply, if the direction is just a degree wrong, the ball tends to land few hundred meters away from its destination.

Similarly, if we are not able to focus on our key projects and keep getting swayed by every possible distraction, then today it might seem normal, but in the long term, you may end up delaying or not achieving the most important goals in your chosen area of life. Lack of focus shows its negative impact in almost all areas of your life from your work, relationship, finances, personal, health etc.

If you are not able to focus on the work assigned you might fail to deliver the outcome in the required time, and this will make you feel an emotional dent in your confidence. You start second-guessing yourself and feel doubtful about your capabilities and this will affect your credibility and reputation in the organization you work for.

If you are an entrepreneur, your clients or customers will not get satisfied with your work and in the long run, you might lose out in the profits and general performance of the business. Due to lack of focus in your work, you will not be able to give the quality product or service deliverable. At times, you won't be able to meet the deadlines given to you for the assigned work. These are really negative indications from your professional reputation perspective.

You would agree that one-off glitches in performance might still be acceptable, as to err is human. But if lack of quality or delay in delivery becomes a regular feature, then it can have a very adverse impact on your career or business or whatever you do for your living.

Not being able to concentrate and deliver your work not only affects your work-life, but also spreads its wings in other areas of your life. You will always feel like a sword hanging over your head due to pending works or due to bad quality deliverables from your bosses or your clients. It will cause you to have stress and anxiety, which then forms a vicious circle. That means that the additional stress and anxiety will not let you devote your complete attention to the work. All this leads to affecting you mentally and physically and may give rise to ailments.

How Can You Effectively Handle Your Relationship Well, If You Are Always In the State Of Anxiety?

Of Course, the stress and anxiety of not being able to attend to your important work will strongly disturb your feelings while handling relationships. Consider a stressful work day of our life and check out your discussions with your girlfriend, spouse or your kids (if you have).

Surely, it wouldn't have been a good experience, right?

All this will take a toll on your personal life. It will badly affect your outlook towards the life. You will see that the lack of focus on your important deliverables always keeps your mind stuck in the unfinished work. You don't find any difference between a work day and a weekend, because the uncompleted work is in your head every day like a hanging sword.

The stress of incomplete tasks takes most of your attention, even if you are watching a movie with your family over the weekend. This is my personal experience of working in the corporate world that if sometimes you leave office on Friday evening leaving some important work to be handled on Monday, it adversely affects the quality of your life over the weekend.

All this sounds scary, right?

But that was not the idea.

It was just to revalidate the point that inability to focus is something, which is a serious issue. This might appear smaller at the initial stages, but becomes a monster and difficult to handle, if not addressed properly.

However, don't worry.

This book is written solely for the purpose of helping you to master your attention and beat distractions by following the proven strategies. I have personally implemented most of the tactics and improved the quality of my work significantly in the corporate world as well as in writing multiple books in a short period of time.

How Would This Book Help You To Master Your Focus?

Okay, it's time to tune into WII-FM Radio Station.

Yes, the most favorite FM Radio station in the world is WIIFM. For those not aware WIIFM is an acronym, which stands for "What's In It for ME"

So, you must be wondering what all is there in this book?

Rest Assured, I have written this book with a clear objective of helping you by offering all those tactics, which are easy to implement. If you develop some discipline and implement whatever tool suits you best, you would surely see a significant surge in your focus muscle.

Let me briefly run you through the structure of this book.

This book firstly goes deeper into the human psychological aspects of why you do what you do. If you put your efforts in getting clarity about your deeper psychological reasons behind your actions, you would be much better equipped to make the desired changes faster.

As Tony Robbins has rightly stated:

"80% of Success is psychology and 20 % is mechanics"

So, this book goes in a well-structured and sequential way to cover the following.

a. You will see how Focus has helped Billionaires to set up great businesses around the world needs. You will realize that you can achieve massive growth in all areas of your life, if you don't allow the distractions and put efforts in building your focus muscle.

b. You will learn the top reasons why people fail to stay focussed in different areas of their life. This chapter is built on the premise that everyone has personal reasons for his or her action or inaction. So, you would be able to identify your own reason. At times, you get overwhelmed with the mere number of items coming in front of you simultaneously. This generally results in you ending up doing nothing significant and decide NOT TO DECIDE anything. So this chapter will try to work like peeling off an onion i.e. you will be able to know your deeper reasons for not being able to focus. And believe me; understanding the reasons is the very first step before you can expect any kind of change in your life.

c. Finally, this action guide will shower upon you 21 practical and proven strategies to build your focus muscle. This chapter is full of action oriented. These techniques have helped thousands of people around already to bring in laser sharp focus in their lives. As stated earlier, I have personally immensely benefitted from the tools covered in this book.

So this is the straightforward and easy to follow structure with a prime focus on the actionable tactics and not to beef up pages with non-essential details. You simply need to try what works best for you and get to enjoy the benefits.

Why Should You Read The Book?

The reason why you should pay attention to this book is very straight forward.

One must always learn from someone who has gone through that path. You don't learn swimming from a person who can't cross a lap of swimming pool in one go, right? So same applies here. You would learn to develop focus from someone, who has tested and implemented it personally and moved ahead. And yes, I have tested the principles stated in this book to build my focus muscles. The principles stated in this book have helped me stay fixated on my deliverables and produce results.

But let me be very candid here. I am not an expert but rather a fellow traveler on this path. The only difference is that I feel I have traveled little earlier and reached a little farther. That's why I feel myself suitably qualified to tell the pitfalls on the way and how to effectively overcome those. Through this book, I am presenting before you the time tested principles backed by science and research with my own perspective and fully supported by personal experience while implementing these measure to strengthen my own focus.

I am convinced that after reading this book, you would be able to chart out your exact reasons for lack of focus. I am also equally convinced that the timeless principles and strategies will help you to massively build your focus, to help you work smarter and get more things done in less time.

So, with that brief introduction, let's get started on our journey.

*****

PART II: FOCUS- YOUR ULTIMATE ASSET

*****

Focus Builds Empires

"Concentrate all your thoughts upon the work at hand. The sun's rays do not burn until brought to focus"~ Alexander Graham Bell

It was winter of 1974.

The young Harvard student Bill Gates looked at some magazine, which showcased Altair, the world's first personal computer in making. He immediately realized that there was a real big opportunity for creating a software program for this personal computer and he probably wasn't aware that he was going to be part of creating history.

He immediately decided along with his friend Paul Allen that it is worth spending some time on developing an operating system to operate the first personal computer. So he opted to drop everything else (including preparation for his exams) and to dedicate full 8 weeks to develop the code for the new operating system. Now for the next eight weeks, both of them embarked on a journey of writing the complex software code that would change the nature of the computer industry.

The world knows Bill about his insights and boldness, but there had been recent interviews and book mentions including from Walter Isaacson (who has written biographies of Steve Jobs, Albert Einstein, and Benjamin Franklin), where it was highlighted that besides the above traits, he possessed another great characteristic. It was his ability to focus on the things with great intensity and for much longer time. He had a great ability to focus on any particular thing for long hours without any distractions. It happened numerous times that he slept on the keyboard while writing the codes for the software. Then he used to wake up after a couple of hours to immediately start working on the project.

His colleague Paul Allen mentioned that Bills' ability to focus on anything for such longer hours as "prodigious feat of concentration". In his book, The Innovators, Isaacson later summarized Gates's unique tendency toward depth and ability to focus deeply as one trait that differentiated Bill Gates from Paul Allen.

And the result is in front of all of us. With his ability to focus and work deeply on anything specific, he generated a billion dollar industry in less than a semester.

Below quote from Bruce Lee aptly applies here:

"The successful Warrior is the average man with laser-like focus"~ Bruce Lee

That's the power of Undivided Focus.

Everyone wants to get that level of Mastery, but very few get there. And the rewards are immense, undoubtedly. So the moral of the above story is that if you have a compelling reason to do something, it brings the commitment to that work. With these ingredients of compelling reason and commitment, the laser sharp focus on your goals makes it possible for you to achieve your goals and at a faster pace too.

The Significance of Focus

If you have picked up this book after reading its title, it means that you already realize the importance of focus in our day to day affairs. However, in this chapter, we will quickly summarise the different ways in which focus can help us lead better lives.

I wish to re-emphasize that this book is more of a practical tool and an action- guide, so the main focus of this book will be towards giving you optimal solutions and action steps to master your focus and minimise attention. Moreover, the significance of deep focus doesn't require much elaboration and therefore, we would briefly cover the major benefits of enhanced focus in this chapter before we move forward to the main section of this book which is the practical tools.

What is Focus?

Let's start quickly to see the definitions of Focus and have a quick look at few quotes on focus. The simple meaning of focus is the ability to pay particular attention to and concentrate on any specific object or activity for a longer time.

In fact, the term FOCUS in itself is stated as an Acronym.

- **F**ollow
- **O**ne
- **C**ourse
- **U**ntil
- **S**uccess

What a great way to define FOCUS!

Some Notable Quotes on Focus

"Do not many of us who fail to achieve big things fail because we lack concentration – the art of concentrating the mind on things to be done at the proper time and to the exclusion of everything else? ~ John D. Rockefeller

"The sun's energy warms the world. But when you focus it through a magnifying glass it can start a fire. The focus is so powerful!" ~ Alan Pariser

"Focus means eliminating distractions, not just from other people, but the things we do to distract ourselves." ~Catherine Pulsifer

You see, the focus is so powerful. Let's briefly look at few key benefits of building focus in our lives.

Benefits of Focus

1. Focus Reduces Stress and Anxiety

Take any area of your life.

It could be your office, your home, your children, your finances, your health or any other important area of your life. If you are unable to pay the required attention to that area, it starts suffering. If you continue to keep getting distracted by anything which comes in between, you are inviting a heap of work to be stocked in that area. If you don't focus on your work, it gets stacked, which makes you sit late at your workplace or you have to bring the work back to home. If you don't focus or track your kid's progress in the school, you get stressed whether your kid will be getting good grades in the class. If you are a college student or pursuing any course along with your vocation, any lack of focus accumulates you with loads of study material to be finished in a shorter period of time.

So, all of this results in a feeling of overwhelm and frustration.

So here focus plays a key role. It helps you to direct your entire concentration on the work at hand.

With entire concentration given on any particular activity, it enables you to finish the work much faster. If you can keep your distraction at bay for a longer period of times, then you would minimize the number of unfinished tasks at any point in time.

The whole stress and anxiety arise from the open loop, which is created by the unfinished tasks at hand. But with enhanced focus, you would be finishing most of your tasks or mini-tasks more often, which will help you to reduce stress and anxiety on your work.

2: Focus Strengthens Creativity

It is noted that creativity requires at times wandering in nature without focussing much attention on anything specific.[1] However, we are talking about the state when you have identified your best creative idea to work upon.

After getting clarity about what you have to work upon, you need to get going and create on that idea. You need to give shape to that idea, put it out to the world and to make your intangible intellectual thought process visible in the form concrete tangible work product.

---

[1] http://creativesomething.net/post/40256760716/how-focus-affects-creativity

Let's try to understand this by some example.

I had personally experienced this many times in the corporate world and I think that you too might have experienced below in your work life.

Suppose you have to start working on some new project or activity or take up something left from the previous day. The initial 15 minutes or so are the real hurdles, but once you dedicate yourself to maintain focus during that period, your mind starts getting in the state of flow.

In positive psychology, flow, also known as the zone, is the mental state of operation in which a person performing an activity is fully immersed in a feeling of energized focus, full involvement, and enjoyment in the process of the activity.

I am not talking about creativity in the sense, which is applicable to only artists, who create some form of art in the form of picture, music or literature.

Creativity applies to anyone who creates anything.

If you prepare an email response stating an action plan or steps for resolving an arduous and complex problem; that requires creativity. You need to find a structure of email response and the flow of language to properly communicate your thought process. Even engineers, accountants or lawyers, who are described as professions with a high level of technical skills, need to be creative in their approach to offering the solution.

- An engineer's creativity is reflected in his maps or diagrams stating the architecture of a building or coding of software.
- A professor's or teachers' creativity is shown in the way he is able to communicate his message to his student.
- A Litigating lawyer's creativity is reflected in the courtroom, with his ability to provide meticulous arguments to safeguard his or her client.

Ideally, creativity is applicable to any human being, as every human being creates in some form or the other and we can comfortably say that focus plays a vital role in enhancing the creativity.

Your brain works in an amazing way to filter out signals that may not be important or relevant to your current work like the colour of shoes a stranger is wearing. This means only factors that are seemingly important will make it to higher levels of thinking, everything else is almost completely ignored from our thoughts; and the brain does all of this without your consciousness having to do any of the work. Only inputs that truly matter make it to a higher level of thinking where they can be further processed.

So our brain circuits are designed in such a way that if we focus on some project for a reasonable period, the neural-pathways start connecting the dots and retrieving all the information stored in it. Therefore, whatever solution is needed for a particular problem, focus brings that in front of the brain, by such neural-pathways association.

3. Focus Gives You Fulfilment

Focus enables the work to be completed from the perspective of quality and given deadlines. If you are focussed on some action, you don't remember the time, as you get into the state of flow, as explained in the previous point. You might recall some of your days, when you are so engrossed in work, that you don't realize how much time has elapsed and this applies to anything you focus on.

For instance, a loving couple sitting on rocks next to the beach is usually so focussed on each other that they completely forget the passing of time.

In fact, focus brings you in the present moment. You are not thinking and re-telecasting your past story, neither are you anxious about what's going to happen in future. So in the present moment, you are simply working on the stuff in your hand.

The studies have proved that you feel more fulfilled when you are in the present moment. Focus brings you totally in the present moment handling the work at your hand. Also, you are most happy when you are totally concentrating your attention on the present moment.

4. Focus Develops confidence

The focus is the enabler for completing the seemingly huge tasks. When you maintain your focus, you start getting internal signals to divide the work into smaller parts; that way you are able to initiate the work in much faster manner.

While the distracted mind gets scared from the huge task, a focussed mind concentrates and is capable to divide the task into smaller parts. As you know, when the task at hand looks smaller, you tend to start quickly and finish those smaller tasks.

Once you start finishing even the smaller tasks, you start to increase your competency in the work and things start appearing easier to you and that is an indication of the confidence.

Confidence simply means that you have a strong inner belief that you can do it and when the mountain starts appearing alike a molehill to you, you have already attained the required confidence. It can then be concluded that building your focus muscle is an instrument for developing your confidence in a much faster manner.

******

That's all for this Part. Though, we can go on and on. But as I stated earlier, the main purpose of this book is to equip you with the necessary weapons in your arsenal so that you can easily beat the distractions and build your focus muscle. Therefore, this chapter was intentionally short to just give you some perspective.

Now, in the next chapter, we will try to understand the most common reasons why people are not able to focus on their important deliverables, before we move to the meaty section of this book i.e. your tools.

So, Let's continue...

PART III: 7 MOST COMMON REASONS WHY PEOPLE CAN'T FOCUS

*****

"One reason so few of us achieve what we truly want is that we never direct our focus; we never concentrate our power. Most people dabble their way through life, never deciding to master anything in particular. " ~Tony Robbins

Who wouldn't want to master attention and build laser sharp focus on important areas of life?

Of course, all of us do want that.

We all know the importance of maintaining focus in life. In the previous chapters, we already understood how lack of focus can adversely impact all aspects of our day to day lives and how mastering focus is so much necessary for the overall growth of a human being.

However, before you jump directly into any learning tactics to build our focus muscle, it is necessary to understand your deeper reasons for your inability to focus. It's only after you understand the precise reasons for your lack of focus that you will be able to apply the right strategy to address the problem.

It is rightly said:

Awareness is like the sun. When it shines on things, they are transformed" ~ Thich Nhat Hanh

As I emphasized earlier that the book is filled with practical and actionable tactics which can be immediately put to use, the strategy that will work better for you depends on your reasons for lack of focus.

Therefore, first of all, let's dwell on few most common reasons why people are not able to focus.

1: Email Distraction:

Mckinsey Global Institute in one of its report concluded based on a survey that most of the employees spend 28% of their working week's time only processing the emails[2]. This processing could be in the form of reading, forwarding or replying to that email.

Thanks to the modern day knowledge work arena and the improved communication means, no one would always require your physical appearance to give you any instructions. The modern day work environment in the corporate culture is very demanding. You are expected to address every email quite urgently. Rather responding to the emails on faster track basis is treated as a virtue in the modern corporate world.

Also, one feels an immediate sense of relief; the moment mail goes out of his or her inbox to others. It gives an instant relaxation that now it is pending with the other person and not with you. Even at the cost of offending some people, it would not be out of place to mention here that email is even used to pass the ball in others court as soon as it enters your inbox.

You might think that it is the one of the highest forms of productivity to instantly revert. The faster turnaround time may appear to you as a sign of

---

[2] http://www.mckinsey.com/industries/high-tech/our-insights/the-social-economy

enhanced performance. In reality, however, it is totally the other way round as it has a tremendously adverse impact on your focus and productivity. The important works and the complex projects require our undivided attention, but every email notification hitting your smart phone in a minute or two is a major source of distraction. Moreover, it is not that every piece of email is directly related to your key project.

Have you ever tried to assess the nature and category of emails you receive?

Generally, a majority of the number of emails will be marked as a copy (CC) to you, in which you just need to be informed and not to do anything. Another category of emails would be your periodic professional or industry related updates. If you seriously examine more than 80% of your email messages can wait for your next chunk of email review (we will come to that 'next chunk' thing in a bit). But since they come along with your 10-20% important notifications (without any discreet difference), you have the tendency to review each and every message, the moment it hits your phone.

Hence, it can be said that you cannot think of focussing on your key deliverable until you totally switch off your phone or train your mind to not get tempted with every such message. Thinking of focussing on your complex and important projects with a high frequency of emails is really a nightmare to address.

The next part of the Book provides very detailed and practical tactics for overcoming the email distraction in various possible scenarios by building some rules or systems to handle your emails effectively.

2: Social Media Distraction:

What do you think about below statements?

- You want to be in touch with friends and relatives more than often.

- You have strong cravings to immediately see the vacation pictures of your friend, the moment he posts on his Facebook or Instagram pages.

- You don't want to miss even a single post on your social media update on any platform i.e. Facebook, twitter or LinkedIn.

- You think that if you don't post a like or comment on Facebook or don't like or re-tweet your friend's post, he or she might treat you as not concerned about him or her.

If you think that any or all of your traits resemble the above, then you are already deeply addicted to social media and this addiction is a major obstacle in maintaining focus on your key deliverables.

Similar to getting distracted by email notification, getting easily distracted by every Facebook, twitter or Instagram beep is another big challenge in mastering your attention.

It would mean that you are in a habit of working only during breaks from social media and the irony is that the main objective of social media companies is to have you addicted to them (it helps to sell their ads to you) and take more and more of your attention. So you can easily imagine how difficult it is going to be, if you have got into the trap of social media.

But don't worry; this chapter is to cover the most common reasons for your inability to focus well. We will cover the tactics in the next chapter to address this aspect as well.

3: Self-Doubt/Lack of Confidence:

You have doubts about your capability and competency and thus do not feel confident enough when discharging your responsibilities. With this kind of feelings or emotions about yourself, you will find it really hard to focus on your work. Every time you try to focus on the work, a fear will start coming in front of your eyes, and shout loudly in your face *"you are not competent enough to do it"*. Thus, you think that you will not be able to do it properly and keep on delaying taking action on the work. You know very well that this has nothing to do with any outside hindrance or obstacle. This is totally the game of your inner mindset. Here you are badly plagued with the negative mindset, which has crippled you to even take the very first step.

Fortunately or unfortunately, we all have got one mind only. If your mind is totally buried deeper into all negativity and self-doubt about your abilities, there is some different work to be done first in your mind, before you even think about building focus. In my book "The 30 Hour Day", I have categorically captured 7 negative mindsets, which kill productivity. You can buy and read the book at amazon.com or else you can download the free chapter on **7 Negative Mindsets Which Kill Your Productivity and How to Replace Them** at my website www.sombathla.com

You must understand that with a mind which is already surrendered to non-stop negative beliefs about yourself, there is no chance that you can think to focus at all.

4. Lack of adequate Sleep:

This might seem harmless, but it is really a big one. There are numerous studies conducted on this subject of sleep deficiency. But the surveys indicate that 20% of the world population is already sleep deprived.[3]

---

[3] http://timesofindia.indiatimes.com/life-style/health-fitness/de-stress/20-percent-people-sleep-deprived-globally-Survey/articleshow/51453627.cms

People tend to feel that sleeping is a kind of a waste of time and think that more they are awake, the more they would be able to work, but they forget that humans are not like machines. The human body and human mind both need rest at specific intervals. You might be thinking that by waking some additional hours, you are going to increase your output. This is not the case and if you are in this category you are living in a total fallacy. You may get some additional time quantity, but the quality will be worse.

I have personally experienced this sometimes and most of the time I had bad days. More particular, if you have to do creative work, this is a big NO. Our bodies and minds are designed to work in a fashion of taking intermittent rest. So if you don't give proper rest to your body, it is not going to give you the optimum results. Your mind will start hallucinating during the days and that's why you are not able to focus on your key projects or complex activities at all.

You can carry out a brief sleep survey about how do you sleep and get your sleep score at https://www.worldsleepsurvey.com/, which is an initiative supported by the University of Oxford.

This survey of few seconds will show some light on your current situation and on what areas you need to work upon.

5: Lack of Exercise:

Our minds are stationed in our body and you must have heard this already since ages.

"A healthy mind stays in a healthy body"

Again you might be thinking (like you think about your sleep) that the time you would spend on moving your body i.e. doing some exercise or body movement is the time you are stealing from your work. But it is like not stopping your vehicle for filling the gas or fuel because you are already getting late to reach your destination. Some of you might think that you are already short of time and where in the world you are going to find time for exercise. However, you are forgetting that our bodies are designed to be moving around and doing the things.

Why would you be requiring your legs, if you had to only sit every time and not move around? It is worth mentioning here that the one thing, which today's technology and inventions have done badly to the mankind is that it has almost killed the requirement of moving your body at all.

Especially for the knowledge workers!

So if you don't want to, it is entirely possible today that you can do everything sitting the whole day. Of course, addressing the nature's call is something which only will make you move (might be someone is trying to invent something for comfort on this front also). So you might not move your body and think this as a luxury but this is a major thief of your health and happiness. In fact, our bodies are not meant for and do not serve us well with such lethargic lifestyle.

Our bodies need to regularly move and keep the internal organs moving. Our brains only get enhanced oxygen supply once the body is moving, as it gives our heart the necessary boost to pump more blood in our bodies and brains. The blood circulation in the body improves and that only supplies the additional oxygen and blood supply to enhance the cognitive capacity of our brains.

If you don't exercise regularly, it will slowly and steadily dampen your brain's cognitive capacity and you won't be able to focus on the things which are important to you.

6. Dissatisfaction with Work or Workplace:

Let's be honest here.

Some of you may not be enjoying the nature or quality of the work assigned to you. If that is the case, forget about focus, you would be just killing your time at your workplace. How can someone focus on something which does not excite him or her?

You need to understand the principle and how it works.

It's either you do what you love or you love what you do and there is no third option.

Please bear in mind; focus comes into play much later, before that you have to have a commitment towards the work.

So seeking about focus in a work which you don't feel excited about is something that needs a different way to get inspired. If the work you do is necessary for your loved one or for your long term career success, then you need to make that as your criterion for building focus on that work. But the fact is, without having a clear reason or rationale behind your work, you will find it very hard to build your focus muscle.

Another related and significant reason for not being able to focus is your physical environment, where you work i.e. your positioning of the desk or sitting arrangement if you go to any workplace. Unless you are senior enough and have the luxury of sitting in a closed cabin, you will have your desk positioned at an open hall along with your other colleagues. If the position of your desk is such that you encounter every passing person and you have to wish him hello, then it is really a tricky game to focus on the important work project you are working upon.

If every minute or two people are passing your desk to grab their coffee or going towards loo, then you cannot focus on your work, unless you put on your head the horse blinders. Also, it might be the case that you work requires handling of tons of paper work and filing. If not managed appropriately, this situation may look like as if you are sitting in the clutter of the files. So maintaining a sharp focus on your work in such situation is also going to be a difficult task.

Therefore, if you think that you love the work but there is some problem in the workplace, then you need to either approach the relevant people to fix the issues or else expedite your search for a different and more conducive workplace, if things don't work out. But the bottom-line is that if you don't love your work specifically or have any problem with the environment at our workplace, it will be very hard to focus on your work.

7: Feeling of Overwhelm:

Some of us have the tendency to see our work fitting in our calendar. The calendar on our computers or any other device we use only generally shows 30 minutes per task by default. You may put the whole day for your assignment.

There are certain projects, however, which take 50-100 hours to get completed and thus you can't immediately see them on the calendar. If you start putting such work on your calendar, i.e. 2 hours per day, it will appear for 25 – 50 days in a row on your calendar. Of course, you would say it is overwhelming.

If you do a little bit of introspection, that is the reason, most people jumpstart their days with emails only. The reason is that email seems to be a shorter piece of work, which you can handle immediately. It also gives a sense of accomplishment, the moment you finish it.

However, if you are part of the bigger project in which you have to meet 20 different people and prepare an analysis of findings of meeting with these different people; that will look like a big project. It would look like an elephant and you are told to eat that elephant. Now you are sitting in a state of overwhelming and trying to figure out where to start from. This puts you in the state of indecision. The more you delay starting, the more you start feeling anxious about not being able to complete in time.

So in such state of mind, it is very difficult to focus on the work at hand.

*****

There could be some other reasons as well, but the ones above are the most common reasons why people are not able to focus. Hope you have identified your primary reasons for your lack of focus. Now I believe the ground is ripe for putting the seeds of strategies and tactics to master your focus in the next chapter. I assure you will enjoy the undivided focus and this will give you the reward of stress-free productivity.

PART IV: 19 PROVEN TACTICS TO STRENGTHEN YOUR FOCUS MUSCLE

*****

Finally, you have reached to the real actionable part of this book to learn proven ways to beat all your distractions and master your focus.

As you already know, it requires a right mindset and positive psychology before you implement any strategy in any area of your life. Unless you have the right mindset and have identified your own inner reasons, your action will be disoriented and scattered. You would move two step further and four steps backward. At times you would feel like you are progressing, but then at other time, you will feel like demoralized and think about quitting.

In the nutshell, everything starts with right mindset. I am convinced that you are now ready to jumpstart your journey to massively build your focus muscles.

So without further ado, let's get into it directly.

1. Set Daily Tasks

One of the most important requirements before you can think of developing your focus muscle is to have clarity on the objectives and outcomes. Every day before you embark your journey to start your day, you must have a specific number of tasks that you want to see marked as completed at the end of the day. It might sound very much obvious, right?

You would say that you do make your to-do-list of what to do and then keep striking off whatever is achieved. But there are lots of drawbacks with the so called 'to-do-list'. I mean, the drawbacks from the perspective of their structuring and also how precisely the items are stated therein.

Let's try to understand the type of to-do-list you make and how setting daily task would be different from your regular <u>To-Do-List</u>.

First, few of you may have the habit of just adding item after item consistently after the previous item in your list. Then you just go on completing each task and start ticking off the items completed. Here is the problem, with such kind of lists. There are no set-triggers for you to achieve certain tasks mandatorily today. These lists don't immediately motivate you, rather some time, these lists just make you feel overwhelmed and stressed by the sheer number of items getting heaped on it.

Secondly, also these sets of to-do-lists are not clear about exact final outcome expected from each action. You might just write meeting with X person on some project without any further details.

But what is the final outcome you want out of this activity?

- Do you go one step further and write about what are the key outcomes expected from the meeting?
- What exact preparations are required from your side before the meeting?
- What precise deliverables might you need to work upon immediately after that?

I intend to highlight that the way some of us prepare our to-do-list, puts all our action items as if all are of equal importance.

Just like putting a stone and a diamond in the same light, right?

So what happens is that by just looking at our to-do-list, which we have made to guide our day to day actions, we fail to get inspired and immediately jump start into action on the main activities. Also, there are chances that you miss out on necessary time and attention, which your important projects deserve.

So here is the strategy to address this issue. You may or may not continue to list out items in your big long list, as usual. But additionally, you should list out those tasks, which must be achieved during each particular day, without fail. These would be such tasks, which you must complete by the end of the day.

So what is so special and different about this list?

Rest assured, you would not add another mundane task of adding one more list to your already filled up busy schedule. Rather be put straight forward, we will do the following.

a. **Important vs. Urgent**: We will take a paper and divide the same into 2 parts with a vertical line in between.

b. **Important:** On the left side, we will list only 3 to 5 tasks for the day, which will help us deliver our most important projects and make us move forward. For each action point, we will have quick sub-bullets of different mini actions required to be completed. For example, for preparing a project report, your action might involve reading some research material on the web, speaking to some of your colleagues to get more information or making a phone call to a friend in the industry, who has some data and then preparing and discussing the report with your stake holder. (If such project is to spread across few days, the number of actions per day need to be stated for the relevant day)

c. **<u>Urgent:</u>** On the right side, we will list those actions, which are urgent to be addressed that day, but on a second priority to our most important tasks listed on the left side. We can work on these urgent activities, by finding time for these activities in between breaks from our important projects or after completing our main activities. You are the best judge to adjust them in your schedule while remembering the key principle that your main activity should be the top most priority.

Mostly, you think that you can handle 10 important projects a day, but practically it does not work in the long term and sustainable manner. You might be able to do it as sprints in the short term period, but you can't continuously do it as a marathon. You will soon feel burned out and would need a longer break to re-energize yourself.

One important point of this tactic is <u>to set your daily action list preferably the night before</u>.

So before winding up your day, just list out the activities, as described above to be addressed the next day. This will help you kick-start your next day immediately on your most important projects. Depending on the nature of assignments going on, you might require quick morning scanning through your email to check that there is no urgent meeting popped up in the morning. But please bear in mind that the objective of this quick email scan is only to ensure that you don't miss anything which requires some urgent action that morning. You shouldn't feel tempted to get engrossed in emails or other notification by compromising your scheduled daily tasks.

The benefit of writing the tasks for the next day in advance is that you don't waste your morning fresh hours in planning. At the max, you will be updating your plan of last evening. But you would quickly start on your key deliverables and will be able to achieve even much before your afternoon, that other people keep struggling to achieve in the whole day.

So the idea is to do it consistently and for a longer duration. Everything counts and adds up.

- Everyday action adds up to the results.
- Every day confidence of completing the tasks adds to the confidence.
- The everyday habit of taking action strengthens your competency.

Less number of daily actions (but related to important outcomes) help you immediately see through the deadline for your each day. That will trigger you to focus on your important action and not to get distracted because you see your goals and the deadlines not few days or week later, but today evening. You are able to achieve results on your important actions, as Parkinson's Principle plays its role here. The Principle states that

"Work expands so as to fill the time available for its completion."

In other words, whatever time you allocate for completing any of your work, you end up finishing the same in that allotted time period. Now your daily tasks have been given the deadline till the end of the day to be finished and the sight of this deadlines helps you to enhance your focus to complete that task. Although this strategy might sound quite simple, you must not forget the words of wisdom as below.

"Simplicity is the ultimate sophistication"~ Leonardo Da Vinci

2. Say NO to Everything In The First Place

"The difference between successful people and really successful people is that really successful people say NO to almost everything"~ Warren Buffet

Seems too harsh at the outset, No?

How can you say NO to everything?

- And more importantly, how can you do so with someone whom, you are accountable to your work?
- How can you do it with your most important clients or customers?
- How can you do it to anyone who you care about?

Yes, it is difficult.

But, if you dig deeper, it is counter-intuitively helpful to you as well as to another person.

Let's try to understand this better.

What kind of person would generally be saying NO to everything?

Two kinds of people!

Either the person is rude and disrespects the others or the person is a really busy one. So I am assuming that you are not in the first category. You don't have to be rude or disrespectful to anyone for any reasons. So, we are talking about the other category of person, who is busy doing things. Let's understand this with the help of an example.

Assume you would write an email to a person who is considered as successful or has achieved a lot in life in his domain. Now you are writing to him seeking his personal help on something. Assuming you don't get a response for few days (it might happen that you don't get a response at all at times). Now, what would you think about the person?

- Would you think the person is a rude one? or
- Would you think that he is really pre-occupied with other important assignments and might have missed or might not have time to revert your email?

Let's admit it. Honestly, you won't expect a response from such person in the first place because you would on your own assume that the person must be too busy to respond to you on one to one basis. So you won't feel that bad if he or she doesn't respond. Rather, take it another way round. If you ever get a response, you will be astonished and very much appreciate his response. Therefore, if you say NO or don't respond to any other persons' communication, it is not that you are acting rude to them. It is simply that you have our own priorities, which you pre-committed to. The other persons understand this well.

If the other person does not understand your urgency or priority despite your explanation, then you don't need to bother at all about such a person. In my book "Master Your Day Design Your Life", I have captured one complete chapter with detailed tactics on how to deal smartly with the outside world. Therefore you don't need to worry about what others will think when you say NO to them. It is only your internal fear or assumption and not that harmful.

But now comes the most important question.

Can you apply this Rule universally for everyone?

Almost Yes! This is because, if you are really determined about your goals and outcomes of your work, chances are that you would have already aligned your commitments with your key stake holders. Your stakeholders could be your reporting manager, your key customers or clients. When your key stakeholders already know that you are working on the key deliverable relevant to them, they won't come to you often.

You will hear from them only if there is some update or change in the plan, which is relevant for necessary adjustments in your work. That's why I said 'Almost' yes. Moreover, these people are the people, who are responsible for your career growth. Anyways, to be precise, you are building your focus muscle to concentrate on and deliver the work deliverables required by this category of people only.

But for all other people, not falling into this category, a straightforward NO is a right answer. The more determined you are towards you commitments, the easier it is for you to say NO to such persons. Only if the task is very much connected with your ongoing important project, you will say YES and include in your schedule, else it goes out straight forward. Period.

As Steve Jobs has rightly quoted:

"It is only by saying "NO" that you can concentrate on the things that are really important"

So this strategy has a great potential to keep away the distractions arising from activities, which are not aligned with your key priorities. Now you can focus deeply on your important tasks.

3. Know Your Compelling Reason

Getting yourself focussed on your significant goals becomes very much easier if you get clarity about one thing.

Your 'compelling reason'!

The compelling reason is that internal force, which makes you committed to doing certain things, no matter what. Once you have figured out your clear 'why' i.e. the compelling reason, your commitment becomes so strong that building focus comes easily as a natural by-product of that.

Just consider below:

If someone's kid's life is at stake, you can't dare ask if he or she is committed enough to do something to save his child's life. Of course, this person is going to be more than 100% committed and thus focussed on whatever is needed to save his child This example, is on the extreme side, which was the subject of someone's life and death. But the point was to explain that your compelling reason is something, which strongly drives and brings your entire focus on your goal and so strongly that any distractions can't come in the way.

Can you figure out your compelling reason of what you wish to achieve?

So before you start worrying about how to master your focus, you need to do introspection and find your deeper reasons behind you take action on your goals. If you are a student, your compelling reason for your studies would be to get good grades and get a job. You would want to see a feeling of pride in your parents' eyes. So, this will automatically pull you towards studies and help you build your focus.

If you work for someone and are deeply motivated to get a promotion or a raise in your job, then your strong reason will be enjoying that feeling of achievement and success. That will make you focussed towards your work in a much-concentrated way.

4. Tame Your Boredom

Cal Newport in his best-selling book "Deep Work: Rules for Focused Success in a Distracted World" has mentioned that while working on your deep work, often time comes when you start feeling bored.

He categorizes every work in two different baskets namely deep work and shallow work. Deep work means the important and time-consuming work which needs a longer period of attention of focus, but not urgent to be done today only. Shallow work means the work like emails, office circulars, notices etc., which doesn't offer any long term rewards for us, but they are generally attached with a tag of urgency.

While doing your deep work, you would get a strong urge to digress from your work and just quickly open a browser to check your social media feeds or make some phone call or anything other than the work. The boredom comes when there is some portion of your project which does not interest you or you may find this overwhelming. But this intermittent boredom is something that needs to start embracing and stay yourself put in the game.

Let's try to understand the functioning of our brains.

Our minds are generally lazy by default. The pre-frontal cortex is the front part of our brains which is primarily responsible for all our deep learning and work requiring greater focus. It requires greater will power and energy to keep this part of brain committed on new things. But once you stay committed and put your brain to work on such boring or overwhelming portion of work, the brain starts to adapt itself.

And then the magic happens.

Your brain by consistent practice for longer hours learns that portion and sends it to a sub-conscious portion of the mind which is responsible for automated actions at a subconscious level. It means that activity, which seemed tough or boring now becomes a part of your automated actions and you no longer need to put mental energy on it, this happens with least efforts on auto-pilot basis.

You must be remembering your old days while learning how to ride a bicycle or driving a car!

Try to recollect how much attention was required in the initial phase to learn each and every activity with deeper amounts of concentration. However, once the process is engraved in our mind at a sub-conscious level, you don't need to think when to push accelerator or when to apply brakes and when to change the transmission gears.

So how can you make it easier to stick to your work, despite getting bored?

There is a way. You should offer a reward to your mind by allocating a specific time for looking at your all kinds of distractions. It could be anything which is outside the scope of your current ongoing important project. It could be your emails, your social media feeds your text messages or talking to your colleague on something. It could be anything to divert your attention from the work.

You are free to decide the frequency and scheduled time for such breaks. You may want to take a break after every hour for 10 minutes or you may want a quick break of 5 minutes after every 30 minutes. Depending upon your work requirements and the expectation from your position, you may choose your block of planned break time. So you have to commit to love your boredom for whatever dedicated period you choose (followed by some instant reward)

Yes, I understand. Initially, it would feel like you are too much controlling yourself. It will happen because of years of conditions of your mind to get distracted by every little sound around. But as I mentioned above on how your brain functions to make the difficult and boring task quite easier, if you allow your pre-frontal cortex to work on the stuff. I have personally tried and implemented this and know that this one art of loving your boredom will immensely help you to beat distractions and master your focus.

It is worth building discipline for handling the boredom to reap the rewards of freedom.

As is rightly said:

"True Freedom is impossible without a mind made free by Discipline"~ Moretime Adler

5: Avoid Multi-Tasking

This advice might sound contradictory to the popular statements in this hyper paced globe.

You must have heard that in this modern highly competitive world, one needs to be able to handle multiple tasks at one point of time.

You are told that you must be able to attend an important client or customer meeting and alongside you are expected to be able to revert to your emails as quickly as possible. You are expected to finish your presentation for that important meeting and alongside you are expected to make those not so significant but urgent phone calls.

In the nutshell, the world is behind you to handle multiple numbers of tasks simultaneously

But one would also argue that a lot of times different things are equally important and need to be handled simultaneously. This might pose the question as to whether or not it would have adverse effects on our careers if we focused on a limited number of things and ignored others.

And the answer is NO.

Rather doing multitasking will affect your career badly.

This needs to be understood better.

<u>According to the late Stanford neuroscientist Clifford Nass</u>, multitasking should really be called "multi-switching," because the human brain does not have the capacity to focus on several tasks at once. If you are multitasking, you are simply switching back and forth between tasks very quickly, which almost always results in a loss of productivity.

Actually speaking, a person who multi tasks is not able to filter irrelevancy. The only objective he or she works for is to handle as many tasks as possible at one point in time. But while doing so, he is unable to filter, whether the task he is doing is actually required to be done immediately or it can wait for some time or if it is required to be done at all.

You can compare your mind with Random Access Memory (RAM) of a computer system. If you open too many applications simultaneously, it will accommodate running few applications. But if you go beyond an extent, it will hang. Similarly, our minds have a limited capacity to focus and pay attention to. If you try to pay attention to two things at one point in time, you won't be able to focus or concentrate on either of those. At the max, you can only club such things where one activity has already become part of your subconscious mind and therefore doesn't require much effort.

Let's take an example here.

If you are driving a car on the highway and are simultaneously talking on the phone with your clients or your boss, both activities require attention. Your mind has to use judgment in both the activities to be able to deliver results. You have to be safe in your driving on the road. Also, you have to be able to meet the expectation of your boss or client. So the mind is not designed to effectively do both the things and there are chances of you faltering in either of the activities. You will compromise the quality of both works.

But take another example of you walking in your office corridor or having a jog in the morning in your residential complex area, at that point of time learning some new skill or academic course or doing the high stake conversation is quite possible. Because walking or jogging in your known areas is already a part of your subconscious mind, which almost happens on the auto pilot basis.

Some people may still have doubts in their mind.

You might argue that you have seen highly successful people doing a large number of tasks at one point of time. Yes, it may look like it, but in reality, they have done huge hard work and the data processing speed of their brain has significantly enhanced. Due to this, they are able to quickly process a huge amount of data, in order to arrive at any decision. So they decide quickly one thing after another, which might seem like multitasking to you, but in effect, it is very sharply focussing on one thing with full focus and attention and completing that activity sooner and then switching to another activity.

Hence there is no such thing as multitasking. You need to concentrate on one task with laser sharp attention. That way, you will build your focus muscle very quickly.

6. Switch to Aeroplane Mode (Solitude Time)

This strategy should be used in the literal sense and also as an analogy too.

You should ideally put your phone in Aeroplane mode for some time during the day. For that limited amount of time. It can be as low as 30 minutes a day or it can go up to 2 hours, depending upon the nature of your work.

Of course at such times, when you don't expect anyone to be contacting you generally.

Besides mobile, you need to put yourself in Aeroplane mode for some time every day. In other words, you should get rid of any kind of distraction for some time dedicated each day. Allow your mind to wander in solitude for some time every day. It could be as less as 15 minutes a day or long like 1-2 hours a day, as your circumstances permit.

The modern day life has really become very hectic and we don't find time to rejuvenate at all. You have long office commute timings, you have endless office email messages and whatever is left, that is already filled with your social media networks and general news updates. With all this, your mind is always in the state of consuming information and processing the same. Even when you sleep with such over thinking mind, the quality of sleep is not that great.

Many studies have corroborated the idea that our mental resources are continuously depleted throughout the day and that various kinds of rest and downtime can both replenish those reserves and increase their volume. During this period of solitude and being with you only, you get to see your thoughts. During this period you disengage with the outside world, but at the same time, you get a chance to connect with your subconscious mind. You must have heard that all the big ideas generated in the minds of people during the period of such solitude. Most senior executives often state that they got their best ideas when they were on vacations. Lots of brilliant ideas took birth under the shower. Newton invented the law of gravity while sitting idle under a tree.

Continuous consumption of information does not make you smarter; rather assimilation of all the information through the processing of mind in the relaxed state makes the whole difference. So go in solitude and give your mind the gift of renewal. This will enhance your focus and quality of work greatly.

7. Create Your Second Mind Outside

David Allen, the author of Best-Selling book "Getting Things Done" categorically states that you don't need more time; rather you need a clear head to think.

One of the biggest enemies to build your focus is clutter going on your head. Take an example of your thoughts going on in your head. You might have an instantaneous stream of thoughts like below.

a. I have to seek a dentist appointment.
b. I need to update myself on those recent professional updates or news to sharpen my knowledge.
c. I have to get some stationary items for my kids while returning home from the office.
d. I am supposed to pay bills online this weekend.
e. I have to get my car serviced in 2 weeks.
f. For travel for office work, I need to arrange tickets and hotel beside preparing for the office meeting.

The list of thoughts going on your heads can be much longer. You may experiment this for 5 minutes and write whatever comes to your mind. Write everything. Everything means every tiny thought. I bet you will be astonished by the amount of data our mind keeps on

processing in short five minutes. There are studies around which state that our minds on an average have around 60000 thoughts every day.
Surprising, no?

Another interesting part is about such thoughts is that more than 95% of these thoughts are continuous repetitions only. So, there is always so much stored in your head, which needs some kind of processing or action on your mind's part. I am borrowing another concept from the book by David Allen, which is called "Open Loop". Open loop means all the thoughts continuously running in our head, which needs some kind of action.

How it works is that if there is any thought in your mind requiring some action, but you cannot take that action currently, then such thoughts keep lurking in our minds until we take action or freeze the scheduling of taking action on that. Therefore, until you assign some logical action or resolution to that, it keeps on reminding you, with the honest objective that you don't miss out taking action on that thought.

It is a helpful exercise on part of our brains (related to popping thought), but it is too distractive, while we are handling some important work. Therefore, until this open loop is closed, we keep on getting distracted.

So what is the solution for this?

Looks like you should have two separate minds, No? Not biologically possible, but psychologically we can take some analogy and create another one.

How?

Let me put it this way.

You need to have another reliable source of a repository of information, where you can store all the ongoing thoughts in your head. But remember, such repository should be such, which you will surely be visitingng on a daily basis while scheduling your daily actions. While putting the information, you also put that required action, outcome, and timelines to complete the activity. And the most important point is that you know in advance that you will be approaching that repository surely every day to check the progress. Now, this is your second mind, which has all the storage data and the necessary action points with timelines. Through this second mind, you have already freed your mind from the stuff, which needs to be acted upon only at some later appropriate stage.

Also, unfortunately, our minds don't distinguish between the high value and the low-value action items. It simply keeps on reminding us intermittently of the action to be done. Therefore, with the additional freedom, focussing on the activity at hand becomes easier, as you have already put all the distracting thoughts in your second mind, retrievable at a future point of time at your disposal. This significantly frees your mind to concentrate on your important activities and you will definitely see a surge in your focus muscle.

If you are not aware, Richard Branson, founder of Virgin Atlantics used to keep a pocket notebook with him always as he didn't want any idea to be missing from his mind, while ensuring that his focus on the activities at hand was not disturbed at all. He believed in the philosophy:

"Ideas don't have time table, so better capture them whenever and wherever they come"

You would have noticed the top executives get ideas on the napkins while meeting with teams or other executives. You should be using lots of post-it slips around your place. Keep a post-it slip pad at your easy disposal and capture your ongoing thoughts in that place, so you could handle that later. Similarly, you could have dry markers, which you could use in your washroom/while under the shower or in any place, where you have glass tables etc. with you. You can scribble around your ideas anywhere. The key point is to capture your ongoing thoughts always at another place to be resorted to later. While this will free your mind to focus on the activity at hand, on the one hand, you will also not miss out any million dollar idea.

8. Follow Technology Shabbat

No one would disagree that the current human age is massively surrounded by the technology. Just a few decades back, we started with having technology only in our rooms and offices, in the form of televisions, computers, phones etc. But now with the enhancement of technology and everyday new inventions, we have technology 24 hours connected with our bodies. We move around with mini-computers in our pockets. We have Google Glass to search or review anything at any point of time clinging to our eyes and heads. Our smartwatches are mounted with technology and again not less than a mini-computer.

And we are not stopping anywhere. The world is now moving towards Internet of things, where all your home appliances etc. can be operated through the internet.

That is the massive growth of technology, isn't? And the modern man is already deep till neck in its grip.

I am not denying in any manner the importance of the technology in our life. In fact, technology has made our lives quite easier and comfortable. But at the same time, we have become too much engrossed with technology for our day to day lives.

The studies[4] have shown that too much of screen time damages the brain. Multiple studies have shown atrophy (shrinkage or loss of tissue volume) in gray matter areas (where "processing" occurs) in internet/gaming addiction. Areas affected included the important frontal lobe, which governs executive functions, such as planning, planning, prioritizing, organizing, and impulse control ("getting stuff done").

So, we all need a break or say 'unplugging' from technology on a regular basis. I got to know recently an interesting concept from Tiffany Shlain an American Filmmaker and founder of Webby Awards, a leading international award honoring excellence on the internet website, films and videos for such unplugging.

Tiffany Shlain follows something called "Technology Shabbat"

---

[4] https://www.psychologytoday.com/blog/mental-wealth/201402/gray-matters-too-much-screen-time-damages-the-brain

If you don't know, Shabbat is the Judaism's day of rest and seventh day of the week, which is celebrated mainly by Jews to exercise their freedom from the regular labors of everyday life and spend time with family.

The Technology Shabbat is a concept which is applied to use of technology by taking a full one day of break from the technology. During the break period, our minds get an opportunity to disconnect with the ongoing work. This helps to bring in the period of rest and looking at life and work from a refreshed perspective.

Shlain states that she and her family follow the technology Shabbat since 2010. They turn off every screen in sight, phones, laptops, TVs, and yes, even Apple watches before dinner on Friday night and take 24 hours to reconnect.

While citing benefits of this, she says, *"It puts my mind into a different mode of thinking. It's supple and allows me to be creative and inspired"*

The idea is that one day a week, you need to get your mind in a different mode, you need to not work. Every week, your brain and your soul need to be reset. Unplugging once or twice in a year on your vacation doesn't meet the requirement of your mind to rejuvenate. Rather, you need to have a weekly practice of getting into a different mode of experiencing the world, which is really important.

Once you get back to your normal world after this one day break, you would start looking at the things with a fresh set of eyes. While it will surely develop your perspective on things, it helps to direct our focus much effectively on things that matter most.

9. Meditation- The Focus Tool

If you ever get a chance to pick the brain of topmost successful entrepreneurs in the world, there is one thing which is very much common amongst those. Fortunately, this brain-picking exercise was done by Tim-Ferriss, in his latest best-seller book called "Tools of Titans", which is a mammoth book with more than 600 pages of wisdom compiled by his more than 200 interviews of the successful entrepreneurs.

He re-affirms that the top most ritual which is common to Billionaires, Icons and world class performers are their daily habit of doing meditation at a specified time period. Our minds need time to reflect on what it has learned during the whole day. The whole day, your mind is bombarded with information of various kinds. It could be the most useful set of information or could be a piece of junk. The relaxation and connecting with you on a daily basis allows your mind time to cohesively process the relevancy of the information.

In fact, I personally tried to see whether I became smarter if I continuously try to consume more and more information. I tried to consume the stuff during my all working hours, but no, it doesn't make you productive. Rather you start feeling lost on what you learned.

The reverse of this is quite true.

If you let your mind to have some time in solitude and sit in the peaceful pose for around 10 minutes a day (put a timer), it can do magic to your cognitive skills. You will see a surge in your focusing power. Please remember that mind in a waking situation works in the Beta level. But to be in a very productive state of mind, you need to let your mind travel in Alpha waves during the day.

Meditation is the bridge or tool between the Beta and Alpha waves. There are many techniques that can put you in alpha waves. But I personally like this 3-2-1 technique of the Silva method to start with. You start with 3 and then enter into 1 through this technique. 3 stands for relaxation of physical body, number 2 leads you to mental relaxation. After that number 1 signifies the plain basic level of the mind.

I have personally experienced this technique and it gives the deepest sense of relaxation and smoothest experiences of meditation I have ever had in my entire life. Therefore I strongly recommend you to experience the centering technique, which is freely available at http://www.silvalifesystem.com/free-lessons

Another helpful resource for meditation I experiment is https://www.headspace.com/, which is available both on iPhone as well as android phones. This is a form of guided meditation and helps you to reach in the deeper layers of your mind. During meditation, you are able to see through your thoughts. So you got to realize that there is something else, which is seeing the thoughts. If you get a moment of flash that you are watching your thoughts, then you have separated yourself from your thoughts. The whole set of problems in the world is due to our not being able to disengage with our thoughts. So now you are in the driver's seat.

What do you do now?

Instead of thought driving you in a wrong direction, you, being a superior power guide your thoughts to go in a different but better direction. With your ability to watch your thoughts, you can easily sift through the distracting thoughts coming to your mind and redirect it to the pre-determined goals or objectives.

You will be able to sit longer without any distraction.

Right now, I am sitting in a cafe, where some regional music is playing, there are tens of people sitting around on the other table and talking. But surprisingly, my fingers are pounding on the keyboards as if I am totally secluded from the world. That's the power of focus. Unfortunately, we don't get it all the time. Our motto is to get such focus most of the time to play our games at the top levels.

So, your distraction doesn't have any strength to overpower you. It is your mind's lower capacity to concentrate, which allows the distractions to overpower you. You would have realized by now that mediation is one of the most powerful tools to build your focus strongly.

10: Do Batching Of Tasks

I can't stop emphasizing anymore that brains have limited willpower and attention. Your objective should be to take the maximum advantage out of that towards our most important activities. This limited amount of willpower should also be used very systematically so that the mind doesn't keep switching between activities of different nature. This drains the mental energy to a great extent.

Here comes the importance of batching of tasks.

Batch processing of tasks is the grouping of similar tasks that require similar resources in order to streamline their completion.

- For example, you should put your high importance activities i.e. making some report or presentation, attending to a call on important projects etc. in one batch of time. Generally, the morning times are better for doing this batch of activities.

- Similarly, you should batch your email review and general professional update stuff in one batch. In the other batch, you can check your social media feeds, your news update, your blog review etc.

- Your online bill payments of utilities or any personal communications etc. could be put in one separate batch.

You may also consider batching on any other parameters.

Like you may put all the activities, for which you are directly accountable to your reporting manager in one basket. Similarly, if you have people reporting to you, you can put their work related matters in a separate batch. You can make different batching categories, like general knowledge update, professional updates, general social media connection updates etc.

I just shared few examples. You can do batching as per your own judgement and understanding of the nature of work.

But what is the benefit of batching of tasks?

By batching, our mind comes into a state of flow. It knows that the nature of activities is similar, so it does not have to do a multiple switching between different kinds of tasks. This helps to increase the pace of your delivery as well because of similar nature of your work. Batching helps your mind to become clearer. You don't have any distracting thoughts about every other mundane job because you have already scheduled the job in the relevant batching category. But the moot point here is that you should be able to avoid the drainage of a finite amount of energy and willpower of your mind by presenting similar nature of work to mind for certain stretch of time. This will help you to focus better on activities at hand and enhance your productivity.

11. Effectively Handle Your Emails

Every new email hitting your mail box might have some instant reward or some immediate action point to be addressed. Also, any such mail might have a tag of super-urgent, but you cannot know that until your open and read that message.

Seems right?

So you could have an argument that if you delay in opening that other email, you might be missing something very urgent. You might think that delay in responding or taking action on such messages may negatively impact the project you are working on or it may cost dearly to you or your organization from a financial perspective. See, I don't know you personally and also do not know what you do for your living.

But, let me give you some perspective here.

For a moment, I assume that you are into trading of currencies, financial instruments or commodities or any kind of business or trade, where you have to deal with volatility and excessive fluctuation of the market. In that case, your entire business model depends upon getting benefited from this volatility in the market.

Therefore, your observation as above is quite genuine and I understand every ring, beep, alert or any other form of notification is most important for you. In fact, these messages are life-blood and you have to keep yourself fully acquainted with all the market information to take maximum advantage.

In the nutshell, tracking each message probably is one of the most important things you must focus on to carry on such kind of activities. Now for people, who don't fall in the above category each message popping up in your inbox can't always be your top most priority. If you are already working on your most important project or report, then every such message should not immediately take away all your attention barring few exceptions. For example, there could be an email in relation to the same project, which you have been working on, so you have to address that email on a priority basis. In fact, that is the part of your ongoing project.

Therefore without denigrating the significance of the email, but realizing that all emails are not equal in importance, we should follow some easy to adapt tactics to minimise this distraction.

Here you go:

A. Limit your frequency of checking emails.

First and foremost, there is a requirement to build some discipline in your email checking habits. You need to set up the frequency of checking your emails. If you are too addicted to looking at each and every message the moment it touches your phone, then you may increase the frequency of such tracking. As explained above, unless your work demands instant response like a trader or stock broker, you can set the frequency of watching your mail at dedicated times during the days.

Ideally, you should set 2-3 times frequency per day to check your email i.e. there can be a gap of 2-3 hours between two email checking sessions. You might think that it is just a couple of seconds to scan through your emails and then you will get back to your most important work.

But practically, it doesn't work that way.

There is a difference between amounts of time devoted vs. attention spread. Of course, your reviewing email message may take few seconds or minutes, but it takes away your attention for some time. The very same attention which was supposed to be sparingly used for your important project has now been scattered. Every time you switch your attention from one work to another work, this switching has a downtime of more than 20 minutes. In fact, there was a study conducted by the University of California, where it was shown that it takes on an average 23 minutes to get back to your original task.

Therefore, you have to control every temptation of looking at your email until your next scheduled time. So this will help you to beat off your distractions and enable you to build your focus.

B. Don't respond to all emails.

Some people have the tendency to add their two cents to each and every email. They think that it is necessary to put their comments in some manner in each email.

But you don't need to respond all the emails hitting your inbox. Most of the emails will be marked a copy to you and it is only for your information, so unless it's necessary to get into the matter, don't respond to such emails. This minor improvement in your email revert habits that will save you tons of time in drafting and reviewing a response and you can quickly get back to your ongoing important projects.

C. Put a process centric approach to email response

Now some of you may have the habit to write one liner quick email responses to every email within the next few minutes or seconds. You get a sigh of relief that the ball is now out of your court and you have to address only once until the other person reverts again. But there is a drawback with this approach. There will be multiple emails exchange for addressing a simple thing.

Let's understand this by an example.

You are required to fix a meeting or con-call on any particular subject. With your normal approach, you would write an email to a person asking for a meeting. Then this person will respond with his suggested time for the meeting. After that, you will check your schedule and revert with a different time for the meeting. Under this approach, even if you have fixed a meeting after a couple of emails exchanged, still there is one more email required to at least apprise the other person about bullet points for discussions. So you would note that under this approach it has taken multiple emails. Now let's talk about a process centric approach.

Under this approach, your first email goes with exact agenda items for discussion with the concerned person. Now instead of simply asking the other persons' availability, you propose at least 3-4 different time slots spread across 2-3 days, on which you or your team is available. You request the other person to tell his availability on such slots. Generally, when some options are given to be chosen from, the other person understands and appreciates your approach and directly communicates his or her availability.

So under this approach, you set the agenda upright, proposed multiple slots and then requested another person to confirm his availability. And in one single email exchange, you achieved your desired objective. It might take 2-3 minutes longer to draft such emails, but in the end, the time and attention span it saves is worth putting extra time. The saved time and attention will help to better focus on your important ongoing projects.

12. Hard Edge Your Work Timings

This might seem practically not possible to most of the people.

First, let me explain what I mean by Hard Edging your work timings. It simply means that you schedule your starting time for the day and end time of the day. Whether you are working or a student, your office or school or college already has pre-scheduled these times for your physical presence in the premises. It means that the organization officially needs you for a specific time on the premises, so you can discharge your role over there i.e. deliver your work deliverables or complete your studies.

People who work in the corporate sector or who work for someone else may complain that while they have the starting time, it is not in their hands most of the time to call it a day at the specified out time. So it means that you have to be in the office at the pre-scheduled time. But for moving out before you call it a day, you are supposed to deliver the work expected of you. Therefore, you would argue that it is difficult to hard edge your exit time.

But here is the thing.

Only if you are not able to complete your work, then you are supposed to stay back for longer hours. Therefore, one can assume that it should not be a regular feature for you not to be able to complete your work. You need to do some introspection to find a deeper psychological reason, which needs to be addressed first. One of the main reasons could be that you get distracted often during the day. You want to enjoy the instant gratification of watching those social media posts or those YouTube videos during your work timings. You love to have a gossip with colleagues about office affairs.

Let's be honest. You might have something in the back of your head that you can spend some extra time in the office late and finish your work. So this laxity in approach that you can spend some extra time later, prompts you to get distracted and makes it difficult for you to focus on your work and leave your workplace at scheduled timings.

I have a friend, who had been working since long in big corporations. But he has made a principle of a dedicated number of hours to be spent in the office. He reaches office early in the office before anyone reaches, generally an hour before. Then he achieves the target of leaving office by 5 p.m. or before on most of the days. Late sitting or delays are just some exceptions in his working life. Now with this psychology, he keeps a clear eye on the watch and tracks his activities. He ensures that all his important deliverables are done before he calls it a day.

Besides enhancing his focus on his day to day work, there are some other side-benefits to this as well, just to list but a few.

a. He never finds traffic on his computation on either side, as he is always before the traffic starts on both times.
b. He enjoys a good jogging in the evening.
c. He is able to spend quality time with his family and have dinner together.
d. He is able to sleep timely, so able to wake up early next morning, to conquer the next day with productivity.

Above is a perfect example of Hard Edging of the Day. It works on the principle called Parkinson principal of time management, as explained earlier in one of the previous points. Just to refresh your memory, the principle states that:

"Work expands so as to fill the time available for its completion."

In other words, if you give yourself a dedicated shorter time for completing your work, you can get that completed within that shorter period. If you have a scarcity of time, your intensity or focus gets multiplied to complete the work in given time period.

13. Kill Perfectionism

Perfectionism means waiting for more than longer to put out your best work to your world. It is due to the fear that there might be some lapse or lacuna in your work. It is waiting to make your work totally flawless;

else you have the fear of getting criticism from people in your surrounding or network. Let's be clear here, I am not in any manner advocating for doing the crap work, which will be disastrous for your career and life in general. However, making the things perfect from every angle and delaying the delivery of your product or service is not a virtue either.

What I am suggesting here is that you should work hard to create an excellent work. Yes, the objective should be to promote the excellence (but not perfection). In fact, there is nothing perfect in this world. And the excellence comes by consistent action and then taking consistent feedback from the outcomes.

The moot point here is that perfectionism is an excuse, which tends to come under the innocent facade that you want to deliver only your greatest work. With this tendency of making your work product perfect, you tend to spend too much time and energy on something, which is good enough to dispatch. This insane desire will take away all your focus and energy, which you can put on other important stuff.

Rather you should follow the concept of JBGE, which means creating a product or services, which is "Just Barely Good Enough". Once your product is out in the world, you will learn by the real experience in terms of people's feedback. Moreover, if your product serves the desired purpose by being JBGE, then the additional time spent on making the product so called 'perfect' is a sheer waste of time and efforts, which you could apply to another important project of yours. Therefore you should get rid of this perfectionism sickness at the soonest. You will see an improvement in your focus and intensity in freezing your work in a fast manner.

14. Reset the People Around

So, now you have embarked upon your journey towards improving your focus. But here is still a challenge. The world is not yet aligned with your plans.

- People will still continue to come to you frequently. They might ask for your company to the water cooler or coffee vending machine in the office corridor to grab a quick coffee.
- If you smoke, some colleague may still want you to have a quick smoke outside, which easily kills your half an hour of your day. And such breaks are generally every 2 hours for such smokers.
- You may still get some calls at your desk extension from some colleague for some random query resolution.

Yes, the world will not change, merely because you have decided to change. Therefore you have to implement some effective strategies to RESET the people. If you had been engaged in entertaining such people in the past frequently, it would be a bit difficult for you in the initial days or weeks. Therefore, you have to now change your approach in handling people, without getting them offended. You have to follow a different approach for a different set of people. Since this issue is to be addressed more particularly related to people working in corporate or team structures, I have addressed this specifically keeping that in mind.

Generally speaking, in any workplace there could be three categories of people, you have to deal with.

A. The first category of people is your immediate reporting manager or persons senior to him or her.
B. The second category comprises of people, who report to you for the work.
C. The third category is the people, who belong to different teams or departments in the organization. They may have a work relationship with you or sometimes it might be just a friendly relationship with those guys.

If you sincerely intend to work on building your focus muscle, you have to be quite intentional about it or else you may slip out very easily and get back to your old normal distracted days.

Let's talk about the **first category of people** i.e. your reporting managers.

This is the most delicate category of people, as they are the people who sign your pay-check and also ensure that you get it consistently. They appraise your performance and are directly responsible for your career growth in the organization. For those who work on their own, this category includes the most important clients, who hire you for your work and pay handsomely to you.

Anyways, you have to keep focused on your work primarily for this category of people, so you have to adhere to each instruction of this category very carefully. It happens that you are continuously flooded with different types of instructions from this category. Sometimes those instructions might appear to be overlapping or contradictory to the previous message. So you have to follow a connection approach for such category of people. In other words, you have to focus on building a connection with your reporting manager. You have to more often visit him or her for the different projects to get a better perspective.

It is not always possible to understand the deeper intent behind a two-liner email. As you know the senior people or bigger clients have 10 things going on simultaneously. They don't have enough time to articulate an email only for your convenience and better understanding and frankly speaking they don't need to. So you should build your courage and confidence to go to your stakeholders and ask the things. You should understand the perspective of the other side and you should tell your reasons as well.

You know speaking happens much faster than email and you got to see the expressions and body language of the person speaking. Now under this approach, you have to spend time and mental energy on building connection and understanding perspective. But with this approach, you understand your work better. Once you have built connections with this category, you can better focus on your work. Further, since you are taking the pain to go and ask your boss about the project, it makes your boss aware that you are already on the job. This way, you don't get unnecessary frequent interruptions and you can build your focus better on the work.

Now let's address the **second category of people**.

Since these people report to you for the work, you need to set the expectations right in the first place with a proper line of communication. A fortnightly meeting in the office and a monthly lunch meeting outside the office is good enough to understand what's going on in the heads of your subordinates. You should empower your team to take a quick decision on the most of the issues. They should know that you are available only for discussing important and tricky issues. This way, you can manage your subordinates and build your focus without much interruption.

The **third category of people** needs to be handled in a subtle manner over a period of time and not abruptly. Sometimes it becomes difficult because you are quite friendly with these guys and saying NO to them becomes difficult.

So follow these few strategies:

a. Use your earphone quite often. You may listen to soft instrumental music if you wish to. This way, the other person might think that you are on a phone call and he or she might not disturb you in the first place.

b. If someone offers to grab a coffee or a quick smoke, you may tell him that you are working on an important presentation to be emailed in next 30 minutes. You can tell them that you would accompany them only after that. And you don't need to join them later all the time.

Shortly, the frequency of them approaching you will get reduced, as they will understand your work-approach in some time.

c.   You may also tell them that you are expecting an important call anytime now, so you can't engage with them immediately.

Adopt these tactics couple of times and you will definitely adjust the behavior of these colleagues. The frequency of such interruption will reduce in some time. Also, they might respect you for your devotion to work. But please don't do it too much or else you will feel secluded in your organization. Use your own judgment as per your own circumstances.

15. Handle Meetings Effectively

If you work in any organization or work as an independent professional providing your services, you cannot avoid meeting people to discuss and progress on the ongoing work assignments. These meetings could be one to one meetings or group meetings. Most of such meetings are not very well-structured. Such meetings have a broad agenda and the discussions generally go haywire unless controlled. Also, on a lighter side, what is generally stated about the meetings is that it is a place where lots of people meet to discuss and then agree about when they would meet next.

The meetings can deliver results only if they are well structured with a defined agenda and a clear timeline to finish the meeting and get back to work. So unless you are conscious enough, you end up wasting your time and efforts in preparing and attending such meetings. We all know time is our limited currency, which we can't ever take back. This wastage of time happens at the cost of other significant works, lying at your desk and which might help you to reach the higher levels of your career.

Sure, you can't avoid all meetings of these meetings even after realizing that how such meetings are huge distractions and kill our ability to focus on significant tasks. However, there are some practical and tested tactics to help you minimise your wastage of time and attention and which saved time, you can direct your focus on other important tasks.

You have to follow below canons of a productive meeting, to the best extent possible, which in itself will give the required results.

a. You should ensure that meeting has a predefined agenda with clear points of discussions. You can't simply get into a meeting to discuss what to discuss. If there is some meeting request coming to your desk, you should politely and firmly ask for the bullet points for discussions and the outcomes expected out of that meeting.

b. Get clarity about the objective to be attained out of that meeting and ensure that all the discussions are relevant to achieving that underlying objective. Be upfront to ask the relevant questions, which are required to get closer to the desired outcome of the meeting.

c. You should know in advance the time duration of the meeting. Therefore, you should pre-schedule another meeting immediately after that meeting. Even if you don't have another outside meeting, schedule a meeting in your calendar with yourself in relation to your other project. Other people can see this later time blocked on your calendar and will understand if you leave at the meeting conclusion time. This way, you would ensure to leave such meeting, if it is going unnecessary longer.

d. If you think that your role is only to provide your details or information in the meeting and you don't need to stay more than that, you should put a habit of excusing yourself out of that meeting as soon as possible.

e. Please ensure to get complete clarity, if there are some expectations of outcome from your side after the meeting.

Therefore following this approach, you would be able to have a focussed approach to the meeting. You would notice that whatever objective you had related to the meeting that is already addressed. You would be able to contribute to the meeting and gain the necessary advantage, without being part of too prolonged meetings. This way you can focus on your other important work immediately after the meeting.

16. Make Sleep Your Best Friend

There is one most important element necessary for mastering your attention and working with a laser sharp focus and this most definitely is your mind.

Yes, it is only your mind which needs to focus on the important things for your career and life in general. In order to shower beams of laser sharp focus, your mind should be totally in the center.

You would have experienced a number of times that if you wake up without getting adequate sleep in the night, you will have a feeling as if your mind is scattered within different portions of your brain. There is a kind of restlessness in mind. Then compare the above feeling with another day, when you woke up fully rested. You will feel that the mind is not fragmented and there is a feeling of centeredness in the mind. You feel a peace and a sense of relaxation.

Now, if you are really sincere about conquering your distractions, you will realize that after fully rested sleep, the mind can focus on things in a much rewarding way. The way our bodies need food for energy and water for keeping ourselves hydrated, a healthy mind requires proper quantity and quality of sleep to function better. So sleep is like food and water for a healthy mind.

Unfortunately, we don't pay that urgent attention to the need of sleep by our minds, as we do, for giving food and water to our body. Despite feeling sleepy, we keep ourselves glued to our cell phones till midnight. The studies have demonstrated that the cognitive capacity of the mind is badly impacted due to sleep deprivation even resulting into loss of memory. A sleep deprived mind often gets into the state of hallucination and impairs the rational decision making.

So, hope you understand the importance of sleep in your journey towards building focus.

Now the key question comes, what is the right amount of sleep you need.

Sleep needs vary across ages and are especially impacted by lifestyle and health. To determine how much sleep you need, it's important to assess not only where you fall on the "sleep needs spectrum," but also to examine what lifestyle factors are affecting the quality and quantity of your sleep such as work schedules and stress. Lots of Studies have been conducted which show that at a different age, the range of sleep to be taken compulsorily varies. National Sleep Foundation in its study[5] regarding sleep time duration and recommendations, came out with below results about the number of hours of sleep requirement at different age groups.

The study panel agreed that, for healthy individuals with normal sleep, the appropriate sleep duration should be as follows:

a. for new-borns between 14 and 17 hours;
b. infants between 12 and 15 hours;
c. toddlers between 11 and 14 hours;
d. pre-schoolers between 10 and 13 hours;
e. school-aged children between 9 and 11 hours;
f. For teenagers between 8 to 10 hours
g. 7 to 9 hours for young adults and adults, and
h. 7 to 8 hours of sleep for older adults.

I have personally tried different time period for a proper sleep ranging between 5 hours to even 9 hours sometimes. While 5 hours seems to be too less and you feel fatigued the whole day. The 9-hour sleep is something makes you feel lazy. Even you start feeling guilty that you wasted too much time sleeping, which you could have put on getting some more work done. I personally find 7 to 7.5 hours is the right requirement for me. But everybody has a different biology. You may work more efficiently by trying different time schedule for you. Try a few and then adopt what works best for you.

How to get a quality sleep?

Deepak Chopra, the author of best-selling book "The Seven Spiritual Laws of Success", suggests some great tips for getting a restful night's sleep as below:

- Eat only a light meal in the evening, before 7:30 if possible.

- Go for a leisurely walk after dinner

- Be in bed by 10 p.m.

- Download your thoughts from the day in a journal before going to bed so that your mind doesn't keep you awake.

Also, in his book "Sleep Smarter", Shawn Stevenson has explained that the timing between 10 pm into 12 midnight is the best to get in your bed. After that time, you find it very difficult to get into the sleep mode.

What is the right temperature for sleep?

For a proper sleep, you have to have an ideal room temperature. In general, the suggested bedroom temperature should be between 60 and 67 degrees Fahrenheit for optimal sleep. Therefore, to improve your focus muscle day by day, you have to work on improving the quantity and quality of your sleep.

This point was so detailed for a specific reason. I have personally realized that once you lose a complete day because of lack of sleep, it is not merely a loss of one day, rather you lose your momentum of the ongoing work. While the real reason was lack of sleep for a bad day, but your mind starts playing all kind of negative emotions in your mind even doubting your self-worth and capability. So, in order to master your focus, you have to get ready the night before and master your sleep from quantity-wise and quality-wise too.

17. Exercise Strengthens Your Focus Muscle

It is well proven by science that exercise is responsible for enhanced cognitive functions of our brains. Further scientists have also discovered lately about an "exercise hormone" called *Irisin* that is also linked to improved health and cognitive function. Truly speaking our body is constructed in such a way that they function well, if we keep them moving regularly.

If you look at your ancestors, they used to do a lot of work physically, as they were either in the agricultural or industrial age. Due to all the physical movement of the body, while on work, they had been comparatively in much better health physically and mentally.

But today, we are in the digital information age and primarily function through our brains, requiring least amount of movement of your body. So you and I are part of a breed called "Knowledge worker", a term coined by a management consultant, Peter F. Drucker.

Nowadays, if you don't want to move your body, you really don't need to. The result, you may end up sitting in front of our laptop screens the whole day on our chairs.

Adding to the woes, you have mini-computers in the form of smart phones, which stay with you always, keeping you totally disconnected from our physical environment and sitting with yourself only. Finally, whatever is left then is consumed by your televisions, which have more than 500 channels at the disposal of your fingers on the remote. So, there is no reason to move your ass for most of the work, if you so wish. An article reported on Fox News report that 30% of the world population is now overweight which is primarily to our habits of not moving the bodies.

There are scientifically proven data to show how you can build your focus by regular exercise.

Precisely, the part of the brain that responds strongly to aerobic exercise is the hippocampus. There have been experiments conducted, which shows that structure of hippocampus increases, once you get fitter physically. <u>Since the hippocampus is at the core of the brain's learning and memory systems, it has memory-boosting effects due to improved cardiovascular fitness.</u>[6]

30-45 minutes of daily time attributed to exercise will help you get your seemingly difficult tasks in much lesser time. You will be able to build a laser sharp focus.

Ideally, it is better that you should find sometime in the early morning before you start your day. This is because, when you get up in the morning, your mind is already refreshed after getting proper sleep in the night. If you can go out in nature, in some community park or garden around your house, that will be much better. Since the quantum of oxygen in the air is much higher in the morning time, this will help you naturally get more oxygen intake in your body and brain.

Also, I have personally experienced a number of times that after coming back from my morning walk or jog, tons of ideas start coming to mind. So exercise definitely enhances a person's creativity and makes you more resourceful, which helps a person to focus longer on their work.

Therefore, if you want to really lead a life with a healthy body and a healthy brain with want to enhance your focus muscle, one has to incorporate exercise mandatorily in your schedule. While there are immense benefits of incorporating this, ignoring exercise for long would adversely affect you in the long run.

18. Optimize Your Temperature

Whether you work in some office, cyber cafes, a student or you are a parent operating from home, you have

---

[6] https://www.psychologytoday.com/blog/the-athletes-way/201404/physical-activity-improves-cognitive-function

some tangible work environment around you, which has the capacity to rattle your focus.

Just on a lighter note, until you reach an enlightened state of being, where the outside noises and inconveniences do not bother you at all, you need to have some reasonable working environment to help you focus on your work and deliver your best. The outside temperature of your work environment should be optimal for you to concentrate on your work. The thumb Rule states that if you are working in a raging temperature, one won't be able to focus. Research shows that if the temperature rises, productivity declines.

Also if temperatures in any working environment are too low they might make someone a little comfortable thus the difficulties in concentrating, therefore you have to maintain an ideal room temperature to work better in any given scenario. Some experts, however, contend that employee productivity is at the greatest when the room temperature is set at around 77 degrees Fahrenheit (25 degrees Celsius).

I am not a technical expert and therefore don't intend to get into too much of technicalities about exact temperature. But ideally, if you are able to maintain the temperature around as stated above, you should be able to focus better on your work, as this works well for me.

Another outside factor is the surrounding noise. Unless you sit in a closed door room, you don't have any control on the surrounding noise level around you. Needless to mention, you won't be able to focus on your work, if you are sitting at a place, which is too noisy. Besides requesting the other colleagues to maintain their noise level lows, you should consider investing in a pair of noise-canceling headphones or ear buds, if you need more silence.

19. Be Ruthless with Social Media

Herbert Marshall McLuhan, a Canadian Professor, and Philosopher states that everything is created by humans to satisfy their needs. Humans wanted to be able to easily travel between different places, so humans invented cars, buses, trains, aeroplane and even space travels. They also needed to speak without necessarily meeting and therefore phones were invented The desire to be connected instantly with the outside world, led to the invention of the internet. The Internet has helped much and now on a click of a button information can be exchanged instantly.

And the next big thing was social media networking, which arose out of the need of human being to easily stay connected with his friends and family.

However, the pace at which different social media networks are picking, it's now beyond the need of social connection only. It is not only limited to Facebook, Twitter or LinkedIn, every day new social media platforms are emerging which are adding to the woes of human beings.It has become a key source of distraction, though it is a boon for marketers, who can now target more eyeballs to steal their attention by luring people with their products and services.Every time you are working on something important, you get to hear some beep or notification, which immediately takes you away from your most important project in the hand.

Ways to Beat Distractions and Stay Focused at Work

I have captured the practical tips to address work related and other distractions in my previous book "Procrastination NO MORE", which helps to better focus on your most important activities.

Below is what I stated as the most effective strategy. Though it is straightforward, it requires you to bring in some discipline in your habits.

How to practically avoid social media distractions?

- *Disabling notification tones and pop-ups and reviewing them after your working hours.*

- Limit your social media to 15-30 minutes a day, may be two times a day in total, for all your social networks. This will be sufficient to keep you updated about the stuff going around.

Some of you may think that you won't be able to control your cravings on your own for such a long period. Then, you may need some 'Guardian" which can restrict your frequency of watching social media, but not getting lost completely into. Fortunately, you can adopt 'few laws, thanks to the technology to help you out by restricting your access to these social media monsters stealing your attention.

Though, it would sound like putting passwords on certain apps, before giving your phone to your kid :). But let's admit, some of us (still kids from inside) really need that to whack our distraction habits.

Here are few desktop/mobile apps, which will be helpful to control your cravings for watching social media beyond the designated time for using.

Stay focusd: you can dedicate the amount of time per day, allowed for watching the social media sites, as you may list in the app.

Cold turkey", which has the similar objective i.e. to block certain sites for the specified number and the dedicated times for you.

Some of you may say that it is easier said than done.

Yes, I understand that.

In fact, I have literally sometimes removed the facebook and LinkedIn apps from my smartphone. Surprisingly, life moved on well. I was able to focus more and better.

I used to check them only on my personal laptop once or twice during the day.

That may be extreme for some of you.

However, If you are thinking of creating something monumental or big to build your career if you want to write your next book or that piece of music or painting for a long time, you need to bring some discipline and commitment in your approach.

At the max, you can increase your social media network watching to 2-3 times only.

But not more than that!

You don't need it. Rather it is taxing. It is curbing your ability to focus on your bigger objectives.

So watch social media only at the dedicated times during the day and you are going to massively build your focus muscle for sure.

******

Thank You!

Before you go, I would like to say thank you for purchasing and reading my book.

You could have picked amongst dozens of other books on this subject, but you took a chance and checked out this one.

So, big thanks for downloading this book and reading all the way to the end.

Now I'd like to ask for a small favor. **Could you please spend a minute or two and leave a review for this book on Amazon?**

This feedback will help me continue to write the kind of Kindle books that help you get results.

And if you loved it, please let us know.

Your Free Gift Bundle:

Did you download your Gift Bundle already?

Click and Download your Free Gift Bundle Below

You can also grab your FREE GIFT BUNDLE through this below URL:

http://sombathla.com/freegiftbundle

About the Author

Som Bathla loves to explore the possibility of personal development in all areas of life. He believes that everyone has the potential of achieving more than one thinks about himself.

He is a strong believer of this quote by Henry Ford *"If you think you can do it, you are right. If you think you can't do it then also you are right"*.

He has practical work experience in the legal domain in the corporate world for more than a decade and a half and he has personally implemented various techniques to improve the productivity at the work place.

He has already written few books on the topics related to productivity, time management, developing resourceful mindsets. He has good plans to continuously create more action guides to help readers to lead a productive and resourceful life (for details visit www.sombathla.com)

He lives in India with his family. While not working, he loves to spend time with his family, traveling and exploring the next best things.

Join Som at his blog at www.sombathla.com and sign up for his ongoing series of resourceful material via email.

More Books by Som Bathla

(All books available at www.amazon.com and also at www.sombathla.com)

1. **Procrastination NO MORE!: 27 Effective Strategies to Stop Procrastination, Increase Productivity and Get Things Done in Less Time**

Procrastination- NO MORE! Is written to comprehensively address the menace of procrastination. It goes on to explain the key reasons, mindset problems and the language, which causes one to procrastinate. The book focuses on mindset development and suggests effective strategies to beat procrastination.

In this **holistic blueprint**:

- You will learn what Procrastination is with real-life examples, you will resonate and relate with.
- How Procrastination is distinctively disastrous, as compared to other philosophies around like **prioritization and Procrastination on Purpose (POP)**.
- You will learn the Procrastinator's code, which procrastinators use to justify procrastination and how to reprogram your mind.

- **5 Mindset Bugs** which rule the Procrastinator's mind and how these differ from a non-procrastinator's mindset with a focus on mindset development.
- **11 key Reasons why People Procrastinate** (You will definitely find yours)
- Lastly, the most actionable portion of this book, **27 time-tested strategies**, implemented by the productivity stars to beat procrastination and rock their performance to the next best level. And how can you learn these strategies?
- Learn the less heard principles like "**Step One-Clarity Rule**" and how to quickly start anything despite feeling overwhelmed.
- You will understand how "**Just in Time**" approach works wonder **instead of "Just in Case"** approach.
- You will learn how to **mitigate digital distractions by 75% instantly** by following practical strategies
- And much more practical and useful action steps.

2. <u>**Master Your Day- Design Your Life: Develop Growth Mindset, Build Routines to Level-Up your Day, Deal Smartly with Outside World and Craft Your Dream Life**</u>

This book on winning your days covers:

- You would learn **what types of mindset** will simply design your days for extreme positivity and productivity.
- Learn the **best rituals** to imbibe in your mind and master your day.
- Schedule **effective daily reminders** for achieving a calm and focused day.
- You will learn the best strategies to deal smartly with outside environment including "**CTT Technique**"
- Learn **how to effectively handle the adverse work pressures** and how to keep going in the face of failures.
- Understand the **3 minutes/3 Hours/3 Days Rule** for getting surrounded with achievers.
- If you are an introvert, no worries, learn how to be "**Selectively Social**"
- Learn the least heard **18:40:60 Rule** for prompting you to become more authentic.
- Learn the **PDF Principle** for enhancing your productivity

3. **The 30 Hour Day: Develop Achiever's Mindset and Habits, Work Smarter and Still Create Time For Things That Matter**

This Productivity Book will help you:

- To feel more **in control of your personal and working life**.

- Provide easy to follow techniques on **how to stop procrastinating** and find a permanent cure to procrastination.
- Feel like **creating few more hours in your day** with simple mental tweaks.
- Work smarter not harder
- Understand **how to be fearless in all situations**.
- Reduce Stress and anxiety
- Learn the ways for **inbox freedom**
- Finding ways to cure your fear of failure and fear of rejection.
- Creating new **healthy and successful mindsets and habits** for life.
- Re-wiring your brain by creating new neuro-pathways to think differently and keep moving further without any stress.

4. **The Quoted Life: 223 Best Inspirational and Motivational Quotes on Success, Mindset, Confidence, Learning, Persistence, Motivation and Happiness**

This book firstly explains the significance of inspirational quotes and motivational quotes in our lives. It explains why these quotes and saying helps us in developing resourceful mindsets and improving confidence. Due to following reasons, these quotes are important:

- These are **originated from our role models**.
- We can relate ourselves
- Consistent reminders of **what is possible**.
- Helps instantly **encounter negative feelings.**
- Daily **mental spark**
- Help creation of new belief System
- Develop new perspective to see the world in an abundant way.

So, if you are looking for your daily dose of motivation and inspiration to get success faster, develop a positive mindset, build-up your confidence, this book is for you. This book will give you one liner quotes on staying persistent, the significance of life long earning and quick phrases on happiness.

For More details and subscribing to the newsletter, please visit www.sombathla.com

Made in the USA
Lexington, KY
27 November 2017